SPHERE

First published in Great Britain in 2025 by Sphere

1 3 5 7 9 10 8 6 4 2

Copyright © Little, Brown Book Group

The moral right of the author has been asserted.

All rights reserved.
No part of this publication may be reproduced, stored in a retrieval system, or transmitted, in any form, or by any means, without the prior permission in writing of the publisher, nor be otherwise circulated in any form of binding or cover other than that in which it is published and without a similar condition including this condition being imposed on the subsequent purchaser.

A CIP catalogue record for this book
is available from the British Library.

ISBN 9781408736272

Illustrations by Ainsley Drew
Design by Heather Ryerson
Edited by Tig Wallace

Printed and bound in Great Britain by Clays Ltd, Elcograf S.p.A.

Papers used by Sphere are from well-managed forests
and other responsible sources.

[Heather: please add FSC responsible sources logo, Cert no: FSC® C104740]

Sphere
An imprint of
Little, Brown Book Group
Carmelite House
50 Victoria Embankment
London EC4Y 0DZ

The authorised representative
in the EEA is
Hachette Ireland
8 Castlecourt Centre, Dublin 15, D15 XTP3, Ireland
(email: info@hbgi.ie)

An Hachette UK Company
www.hachette.co.uk

www.littlebrown.co.uk

For cats and their people.

For Rascal. The world's funniest, cuddliest, most loving cat.

For Sig, Maggie, Grumps, Dave, Wyatt, Nova, and Runt.

For Mittens (2008-2025).
Sweet dreams. 🐾🐾

so soft...

so cute...

you know you want to pet it...

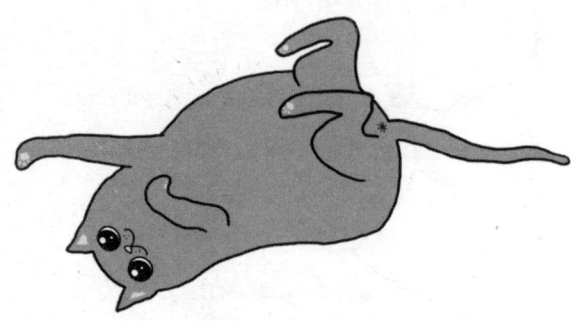

Dear humans, remember that each time
you go in for a belly rub, you roll the dice.
Be greeted with the softest fur...

SURPRISE!
I CHOOSE VIOLENCE!

...or a world of pain.

You're a good parent.
You buy your cat
thoughtful gifts.

You try SO hard.

new favourite toy, the box it came in

luxury alpaca yarn hand-crocheted cat toy, stuffed with 100% organic catnip

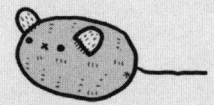

Too hard.

A sunny Sunday with no plans. You finally buy those beautiful plants you've been meaning to get for ages. You get home, lovingly pot them, and take a well-earned five-minute break before doing the rest.

Five minutes later...

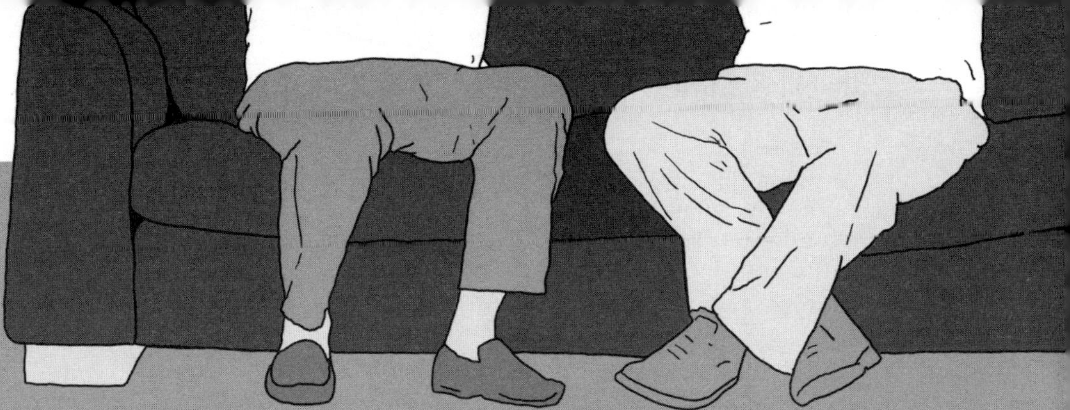

Etiquette dictates that only special guests get to witness the traditional feline welcome.

You must realise that privacy is something you forfeited the moment you invited that furry creature into your home.

Did you like your new carpet?

Cats' claws must be sharpened.

A post designed for exactly this is
a perfect purchase, right? Wrong.

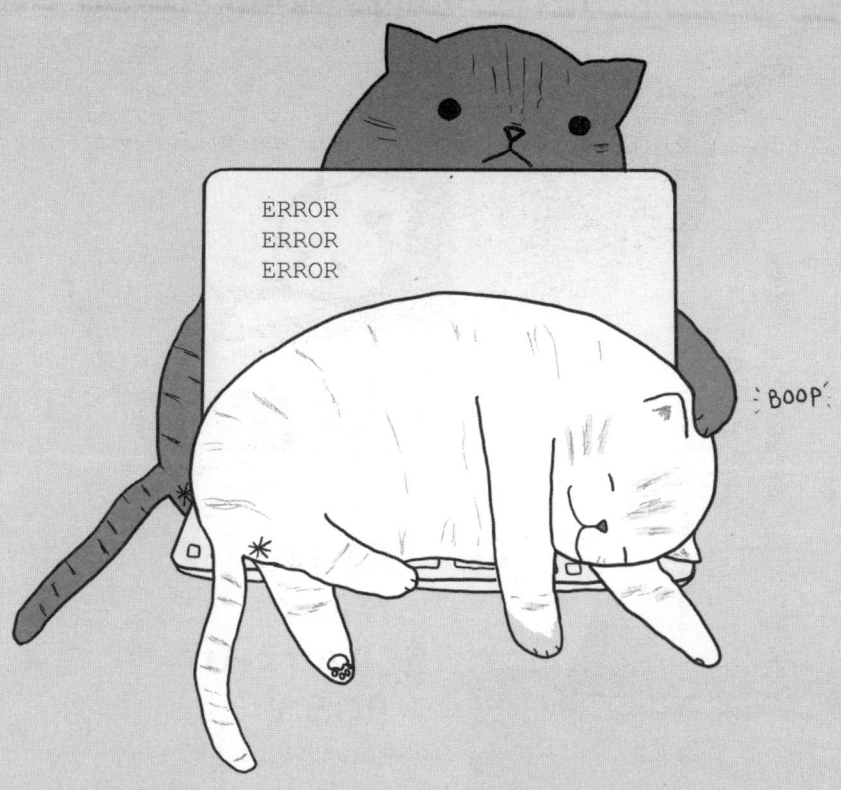

By all means, human, leave your laptop open on something important that you haven't saved.

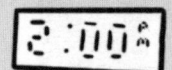

The times when you sleep and the times when your cat sleeps have little in common.

This is my garden now

Your neighbours may also have cats. Understand that they don't take heed of trivial things like fences, or your lovingly cared-for perennials. Nature calls where and when it will.

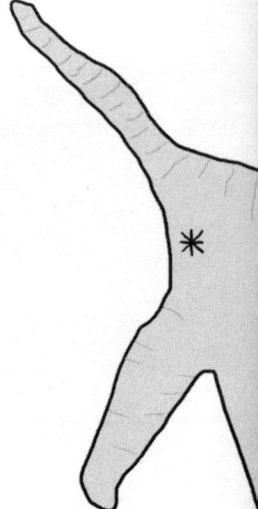

My compliments to the chef

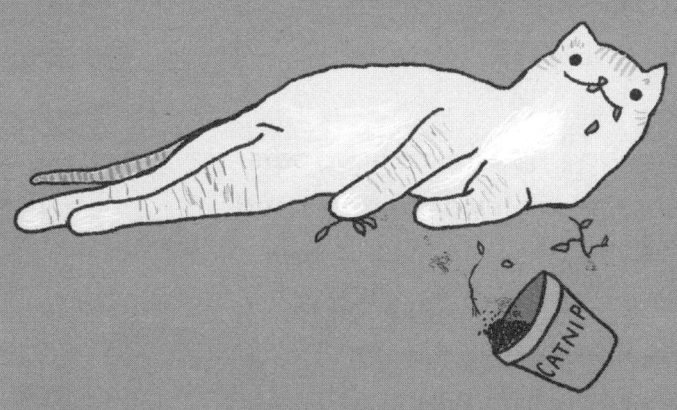

Catnip – for parenting emergencies only.

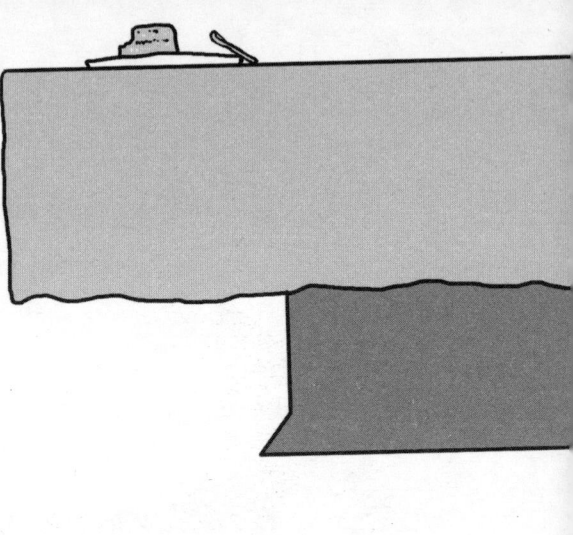

Mine now.

You can't afford help in the house. Your cat will do what it can to clean up leftovers. It is doing *you* a favour.

If you have a senior cat, they must be treated with utmost dignity and respect at all times, or you will pay the price.

Christmas.
A season of joy, festivity and, crucially, gifts.

But for cat parents, great peril accompanies this bounty. So much more to rip and tear and chew. So many delicate things to break.

Most of all,
so much
tree to
climb.

Maybe you bought a cat to keep your house free of mice.

Maybe you made a mistake.

You might be looking for
your cat (why, though?
They want to be left in peace).

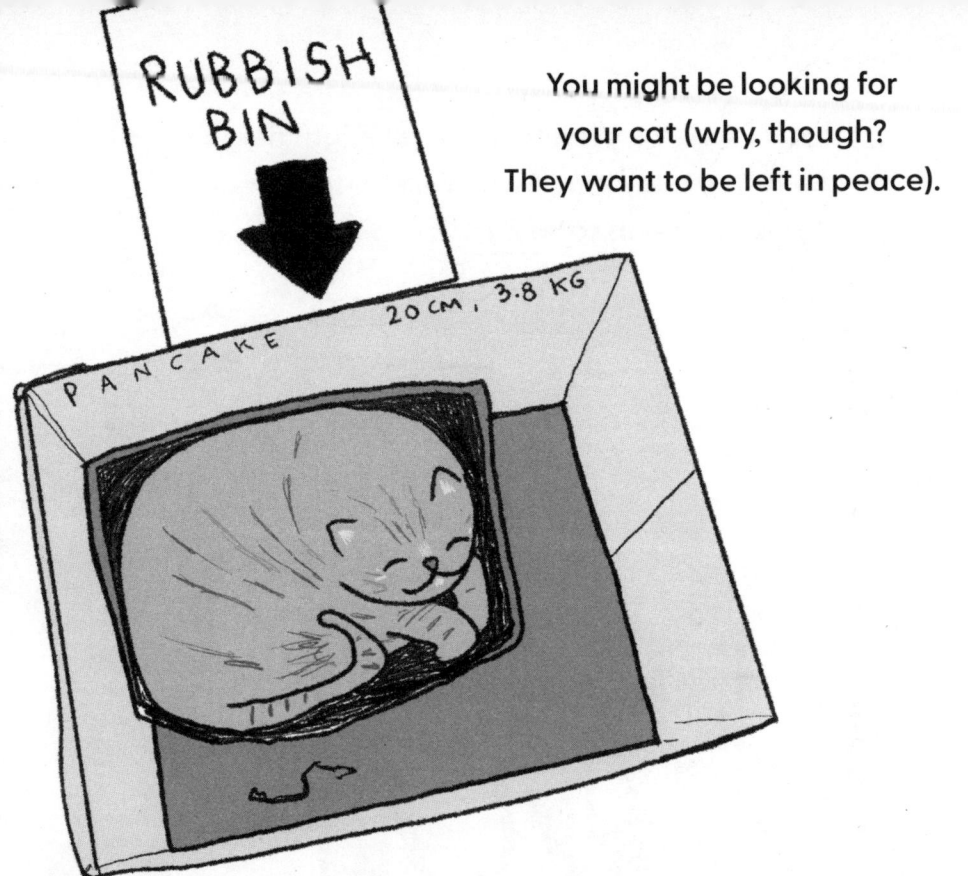

Always look in the least likely place
and there you shall find a cat.

If you work from home, your cat might deign to keep you company. Stay alert to peril – quiet does not mean safety. To you, a data cable...

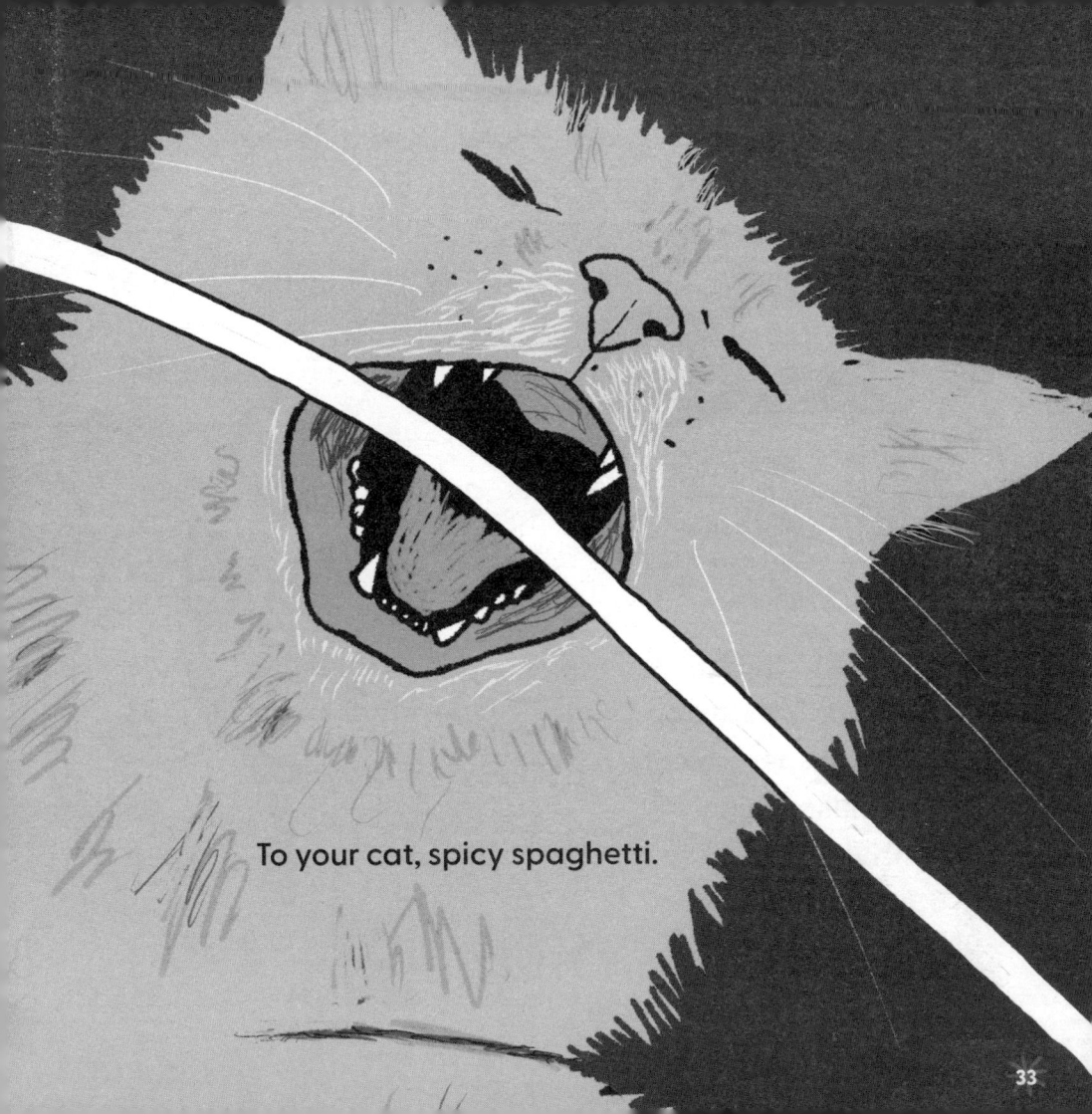

Cats like to spoon just like us, only they also like to whisper violent, appalling, highly offensive things to each other while doing so. This is true cat love.

You want to take photos of your black cats?
Good luck.

To them it's just something to destroy.

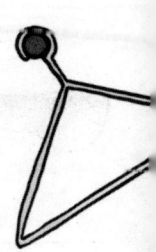

You have a responsibility to serve cats food befitting sleek, apex predators, a species worshipped by ancient civilizations, who just happen to sleep in your home.

Do not disappoint them.

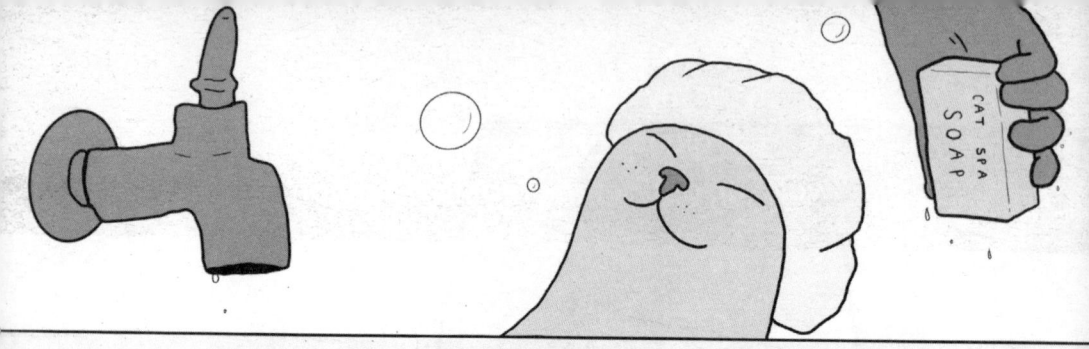

You might try to wash your cat, after a particularly busy night rolling in dirt and fighting foxes.

You will regret it.

You have more than one cat – lucky you! They will go from calm to fighting in the blink of an eye.

Cats deserve good accessories.

Certainly more than you do.

Did you really think the £50 Pets at Home kitty fountain would be any better than the kitchen sink?

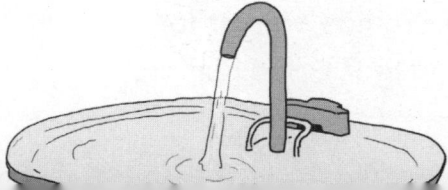

When
will
you
learn?

Cats need stimulation. Provide objects for them to rip and chew and tear. Good human.

Ah yes, you got an indoor cat.

You found a good spot for the litter tray.

Haha, wait, there is no good spot for the litter tray.

Cat-on-cat affection is a true rarity.

Enjoy it, before it flips to unbridled hatred.

If you're a brave (idiotic) soul whose home contains a mixture of cats and dogs, good luck to you.

**Dietary requirements?
Yes, all of them.**

A common ploy to remind you who's in charge.

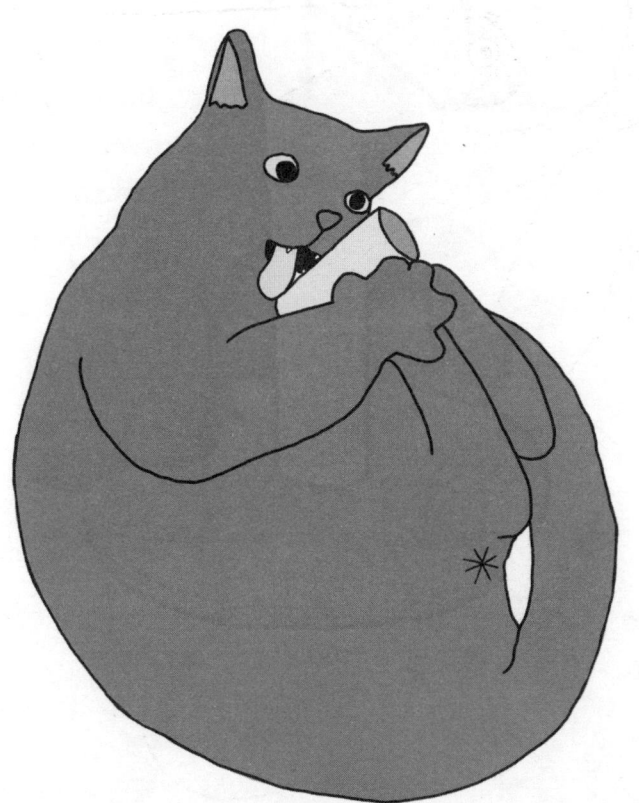

Cat hair is made from a unique substance which has the ability to stick to any clean surface.

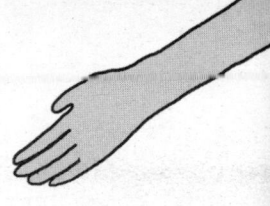

If you DARE to go on holiday, prepare to suffer the consequences when you return.

They have the boredom threshold of a toddler yet can sleep for 18 hours a day.

Your cat maintains the right to refuse.

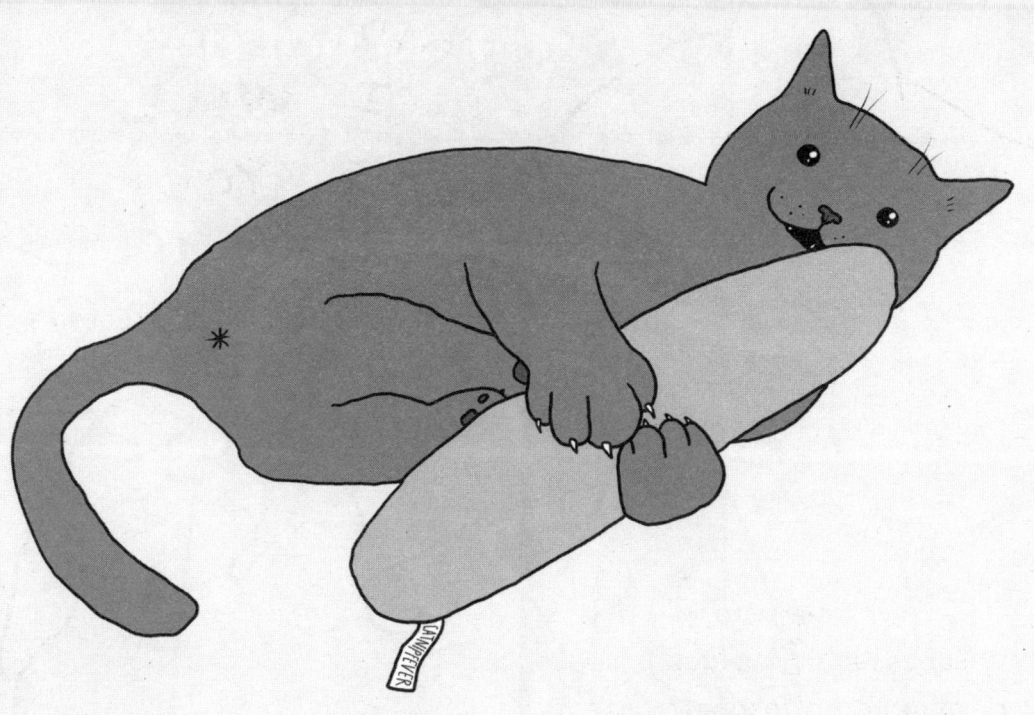

Catnip narcosis is a strange and wonderous thing to witness.

I got this!

I do not got this.

No more will be said about this.

Kittens have evolved the ability to make you love them so they can ruin your soft furnishings without reproach.

Rise and shine. Welcome to your new alarm clock. No snooze, no off button.

Cats are loyal, dependable, proud, agile.
Often, they forget this and act like aloof idiots.

All you wanted was single photo
to show how beautiful your cat is.

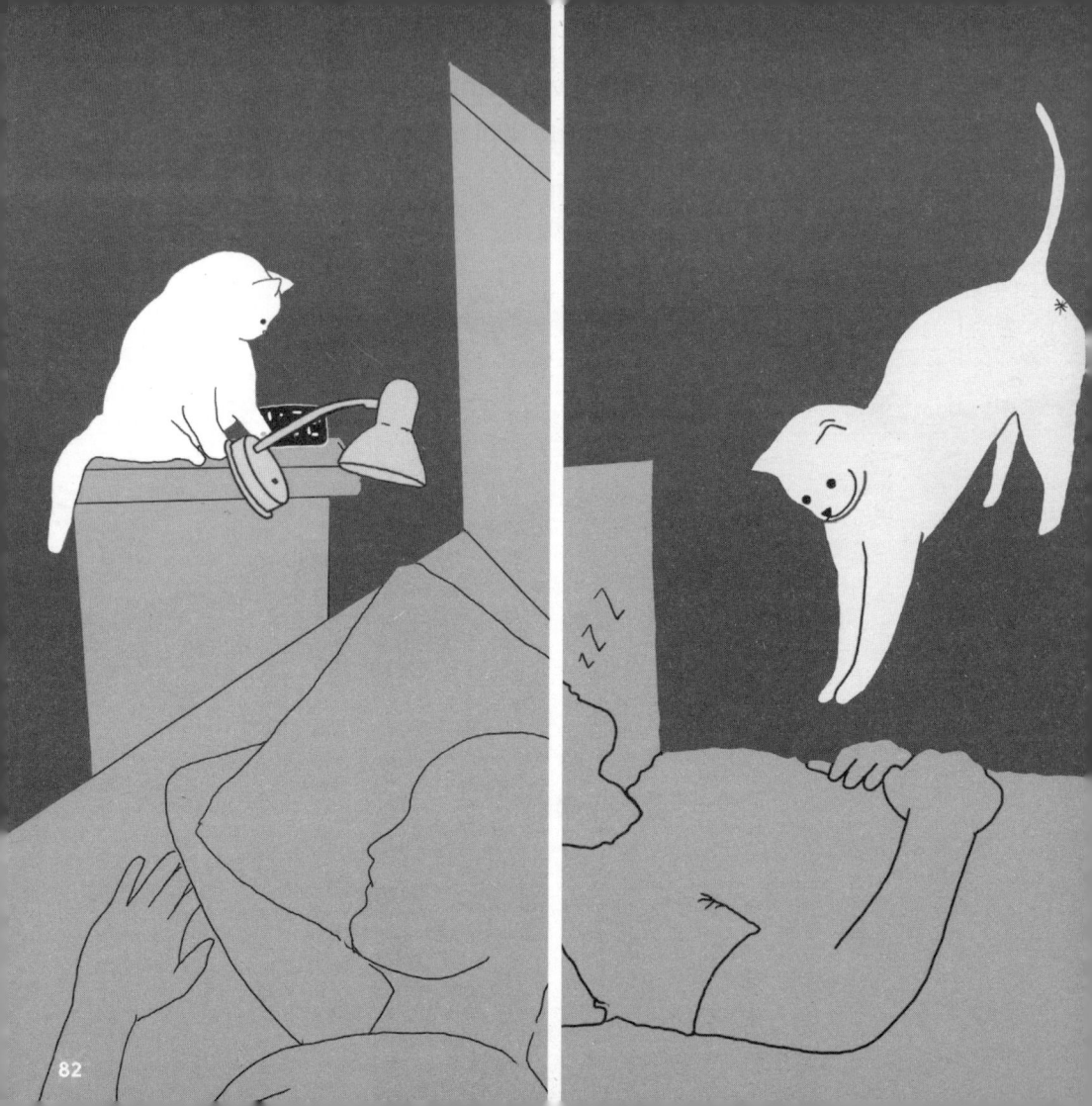

Your bed?
I don't think so.
You are here by
invite only and
your cat can
evict you at
anytime.

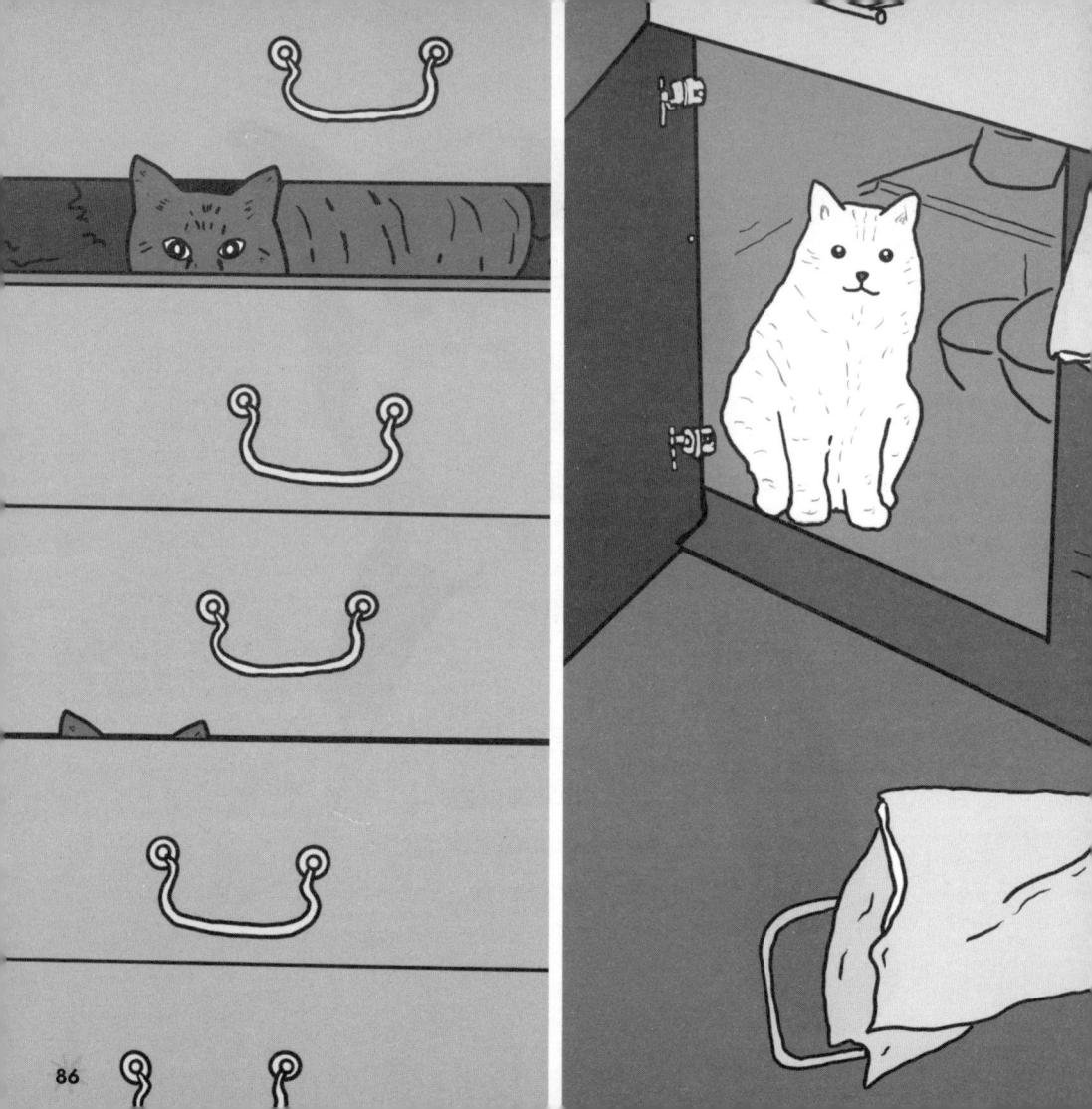

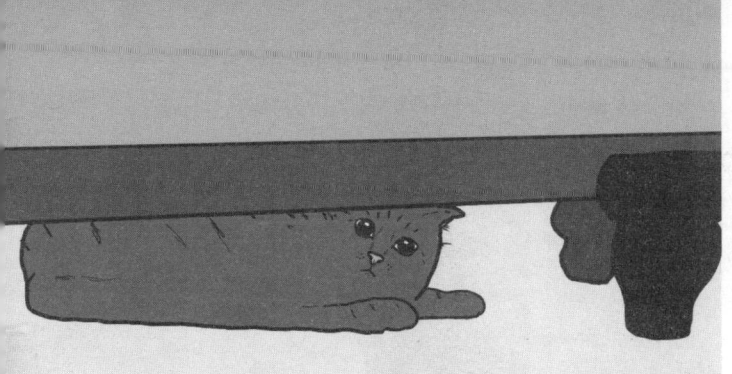

Meanwhile, the cosy, expensive cat beds deposited around the house remain empty, unloved and unused.

You love your pets equally.
Your cat however, holds nothing
but disdain for any competition
for your affections.

Did you really believe they liked each other?

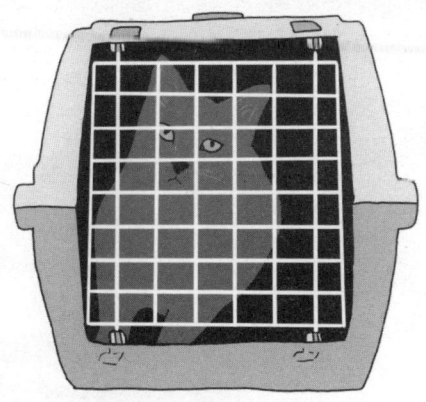

It's been said that Harry Houdini studied vetbound cats for escapology tips.

They convulse.
They retch.
They yowl.
Behold,
a tiny fur ball.

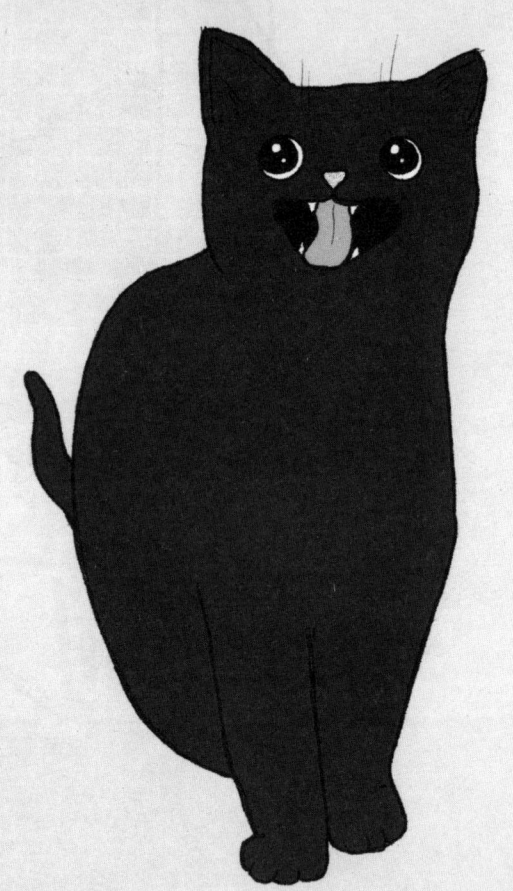

So cute.
But this is just practice before they move on to the stairway carpet.

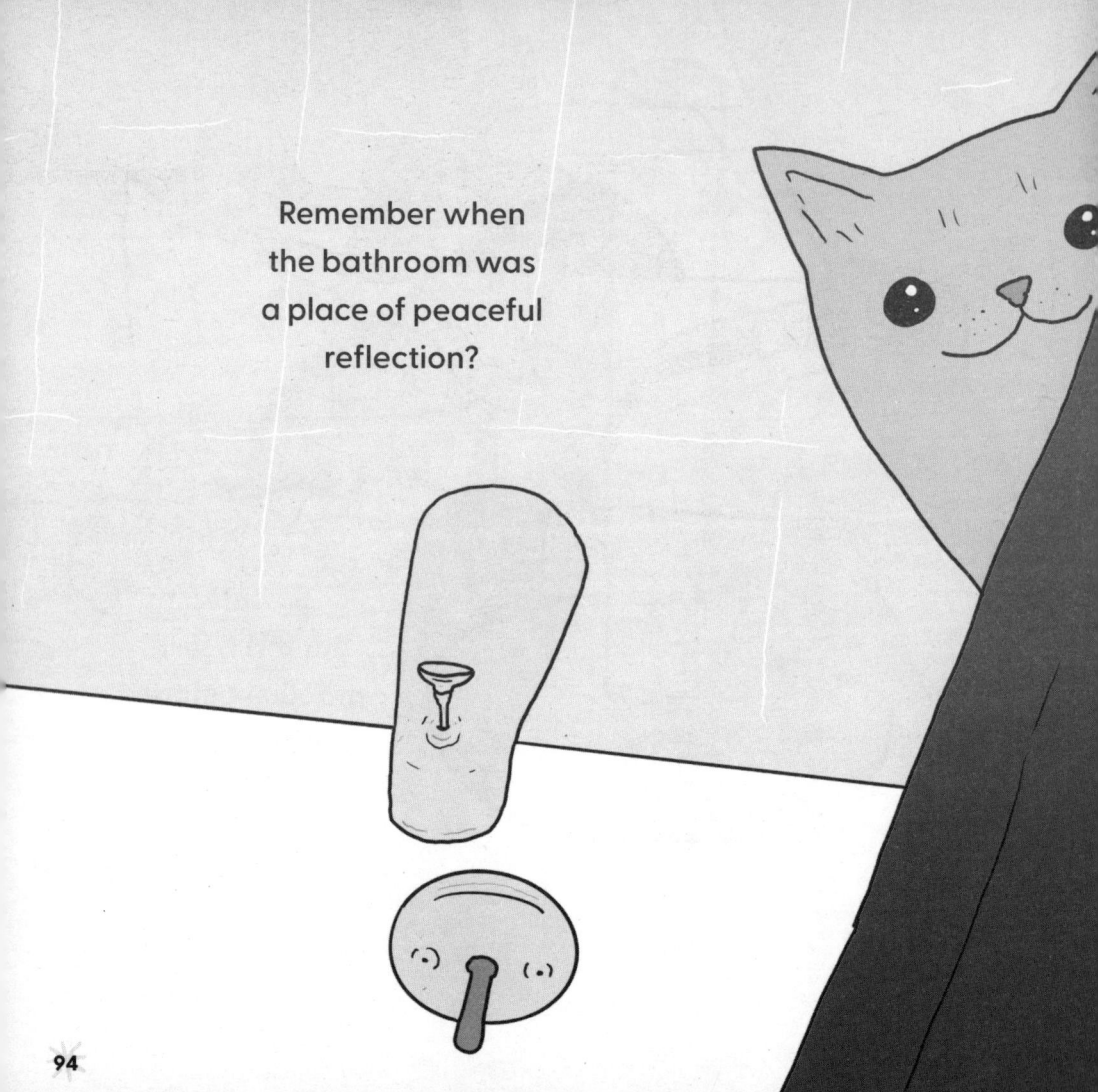

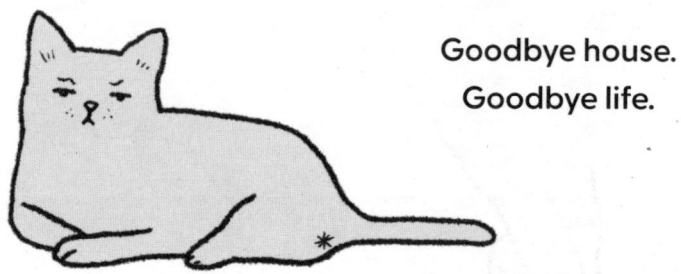

Goodbye house.
Goodbye life.

Please love me.
I promise
you will not
regret it.

So you invited a pedigree
Bengal into your home?

No. You invited Tigger,
after he's eaten all the blue Smarties.

The zoomies can strike at any time, for any reason.
Save your valuables first.

Your cat's instincts for cleanliness and self-care does not extend to your crockery.

Despite waiting eagerly for you to feed them, they will reject whatever you dish up.

Do not take it personally.

Bored indifference. The primary feline emotion.

Cat origami.

Playtime is not fun for everyone.

What could be worse for your unsaved work than a cat that thinks it's a computer engineer.

Household objects are no longer yours.
Whatever use they had before is secondary.

By all means dress your cat for Instagram pics...
If you don't like your fingers.

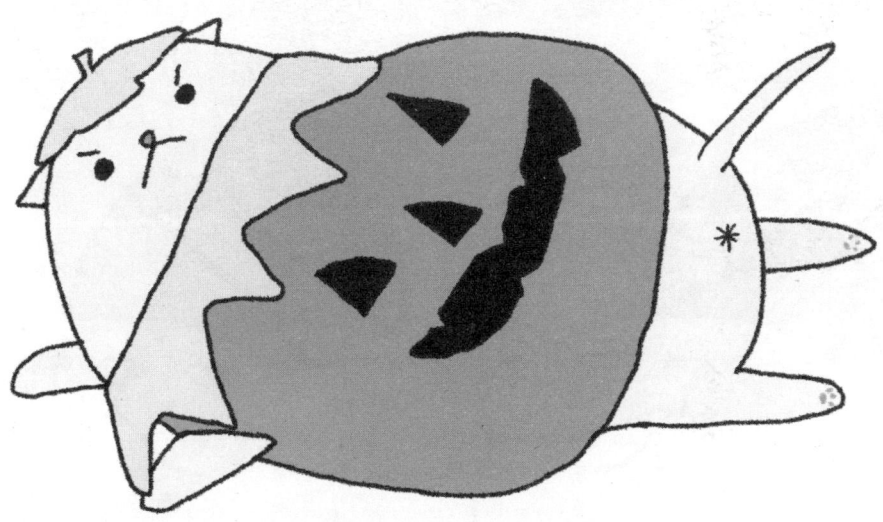

Good luck when you try to undress it.

It takes many scars before you understand cat body language.

ACKNOWLEDGEMENTS

This book wouldn't be possible without a very special set of cats, who graciously served as models. Many thanks to:

Bagel (and human Aimee Kitson) pp. 6-7
Barker and Corbett (and humans Tamsin and Richard Kitson) pp. 8-9
Otis (and human Kirsteen Astor) pp. 10-11
Pluto and Maggie (and humans Sunaina Sherchan, Imogen and Craig Smith) p. 12
Blue Fluff (and human Stephanie Melrose) p. 16
Gumbus (and human Victoria E.) p. 17 and p. 99
Cat (and human Jo Taylor) p. 18
Fitz and Hugo (and human Narges Nojoumi) p. 19
Cobweb (and human Ella Garrett) pp. 20-21
Obama (and human Caitlin Landuyt) p. 22
Margot (and human Katya Ellis) p. 23
Misa (and human Ella Garrett) p. 24
Mittens (and humans Harriet Mann and Jack Butler) p. 25
Mulder and Scully (and human Jenni Hill) pp. 26-27
Mouse (and human Caitriona Row) p. 30
Pancake (and human Abby Marshall) p. 31
Rascal (and human Tig Wallace) pp. 32-33

Harry and Ron (and humans Elias Fasoulas and Aaron Sibley) p. 34
Ruth and Rosie (and human Amanda Keats) p. 35
Ruby (and human Sarah Savitt) pp. 36-37
Marlene Dietrich (and human Olivia Barber) pp. 38-39
Lola (and humans Charlie and Sam Short) p. 43
Zaggy (and human Sophie Davies) pp. 46-47
Ødegaard (and human Bryony Rogers) pp. 60-61
Bea and Milo (and human Molly Walker-Sharp) p. 63
Winky (and human caretakers @winkythedwarfcat) p. 72
Kittens fostered by human Hannah Shaw p. 76
Bear (and human Cassy Nacard) p. 78
Buffy (and human Grace Vincent) p. 79
Shelby (and human Alice Warburton) p. 85
Chou Chou and Littles (and human Andrew Marttila) p. 88
Ferg (and human Andrew Marttila) p. 97
Akila (and human Louise Henderson-Clark) p. 98